OUR LOVE STORY

A KEEPSAKE JOURNAL
FOR COUPLES

THIS JOURNAL BELONGS TO:

_____

&

_____

A LITTLE BIT ABOUT US:

Add a picture here!

THIS IS THE STORY OF

_____ & _____

WE'VE BEEN TOGETHER FOR

_____

HOW TO USE THIS JOURNAL

Are you looking for a fun way to commemorate your relationship and share special memories from your relationship.

In this journal you will find fill in the blank questions on each page for you and your significant other to complete.

Go through each question and add responses to them about your experiences as a couple.

After you finish with this journal, you will have a memorable keepsake that you can pass down and share full of wonderful memories and experiences with your significant other.

Enjoy!

YOU

WHAT DID YOU FIRST NOTICE ABOUT ME?

ME

WHAT DID YOU FIRST NOTICE ABOUT ME?

YOU

WHAT ARE THE TOP 3 QUALITIES YOU LOVE
ABOUT ME THE MOST?

ME

WHAT ARE THE TOP 3 QUALITIES YOU LOVE ABOUT ME THE MOST?

YOU

WHAT WAS YOUR FIRST THOUGHT
WHEN YOU SAW ME?

ME

WHAT WAS YOUR FIRST THOUGHT
WHEN YOU SAW ME?

YOU

WHAT DO YOU THINK ARE MY BEST QUALITIES?

ME

WHAT DO YOU THINK ARE MY BEST QUALITIES?

YOU

WHAT'S SOMETHING THAT I DO THAT MAKES YOU FEEL THE MOST LOVED?

ME

WHAT'S SOMETHING THAT I DO THAT MAKES
YOU FEEL THE MOST LOVED?

YOU

WHAT IS THE BEST PART OF OUR RELATIONSHIP?

ME

WHAT IS THE BEST PART OF OUR RELATIONSHIP?

YOU

WHAT DO YOU THINK IS MY MOST ATTRACTIVE PHYSICAL FEATURE?

ME

WHAT DO YOU THINK IS MY MOST ATTRACTIVE PHYSICAL FEATURE?

HOW MUCH DO YOU THINK WE HAVE EVOLVED
AS A COUPLE FROM WHEN WE FIRST MET?

HOW MUCH DO YOU THINK WE HAVE EVOLVED
AS A COUPLE FROM WHEN WE FIRST MET?

WHICH CELEBRITY DO I RESEMBLE THE MOST?

ME

WHICH CELEBRITY DO I RESEMBLE THE MOST?

YOU

WHAT IS YOUR FAVORITE HOBBY TO
DO WITH ME?

ME

WHAT IS YOUR FAVORITE HOBBY TO
DO WITH ME?

YOU

WHAT DID YOU THINK ABOUT OUR FIRST DATE?

ME

WHAT DID YOU THINK ABOUT OUR FIRST DATE?

IF WE COULD TRAVEL ANYWHERE IN THE
WORLD, WHERE WOULD YOU GO?

ME

IF WE COULD TRAVEL ANYWHERE IN THE WORLD, WHERE WOULD YOU GO?

WHAT IS SOMETHING YOU'VE ALWAYS WANTED TO TRY WITH ME?

ME

WHAT IS SOMETHING YOU'VE ALWAYS WANTED
TO TRY WITH ME?

WHAT IS ONE OF YOUR FAVORITE SONGS OR
MOVIES THAT REMIND YOU OF ME?

ME

WHAT IS ONE OF YOUR FAVORITE SONGS OR
MOVIES THAT REMIND YOU OF ME?

YOU

WHAT TURNS YOU ON THE MOST ABOUT ME?

ME

WHAT TURNS YOU ON THE MOST ABOUT ME?

YOU

WHAT IS THE ONE THING THAT ANNOYS YOU ABOUT ME?

WHAT IS THE ONE THING THAT ANNOYS YOU ABOUT ME?

YOU

WHAT MAKES YOU THE HAPPIEST ABOUT OUR RELATIONSHIP?

ME

WHAT MAKES YOU THE HAPPIEST ABOUT OUR
RELATIONSHIP?

IF WE COULD TRY SOMETHING "NEW" AS A COUPLE, WHAT WOULD IT BE AND WHY?

IF WE COULD TRY SOMETHING "NEW" AS A COUPLE, WHAT WOULD IT BE AND WHY?

YOU

WHAT'S A QUESTION YOU'VE ALWAYS WANTED TO ASK ME BUT NEVER HAVE?

WHAT'S A QUESTION YOU'VE ALWAYS WANTED TO ASK ME BUT NEVER HAVE?

YOU

WHEN DO YOU FEEL RESPECTED BY ME?

ME

WHEN DO YOU FEEL RESPECTED BY ME?

YOU

WHAT IS YOUR FIRST MEMORY OF ME?
DESCRIBE IT IN DETAIL.

ME

WHAT IS YOUR FIRST MEMORY OF ME?
DESCRIBE IT IN DETAIL.

YOU

DESCRIBE ME IN THREE WORDS.

ME

DESCRIBE ME IN THREE WORDS.

YOU

WHAT IS THE FIRST MOVIE WE WATCHED TOGETHER?

WHAT IS THE FIRST MOVIE WE WATCHED TOGETHER?

DESCRIBE OUR FIRST KISS.

DESCRIBE OUR FIRST KISS.

YOU

WHEN DID YOU FIRST FALL IN LOVE WITH ME?

ME

WHEN DID YOU FIRST FALL IN LOVE WITH ME?

YOU

DESCRIBE THE PERFECT DATE NIGHT FOR US.

ME

DESCRIBE THE PERFECT DATE NIGHT FOR US.

YOU

WHAT ABOUT ME STANDS OUT TO YOU THE MOST?

ME

WHAT ABOUT ME STANDS OUT TO YOU
THE MOST?

YOU

WHAT DO YOU CHERISH THE MOST ABOUT YOUR RELATIONSHIP?

WHAT DO YOU CHERISH THE MOST ABOUT YOUR RELATIONSHIP?

YOU

HOW WOULD YOU LIKE TO SPEND YOUR DAYS
AFTER WE AGE?

ME

HOW WOULD YOU LIKE TO SPEND YOUR DAYS AFTER WE AGE?

WHAT DOES IT FEEL LIKE WHEN YOU'RE LAYING NEXT TO ME?

ME

WHAT DOES IT FEEL LIKE WHEN YOU'RE LAYING NEXT TO ME?

YOU

DO YOU BELIEVE WE ARE SOULMATES?

ME

DO YOU BELIEVE WE ARE SOULMATES?

WHAT IS YOUR FAVORITE TYPE OF OUTFIT TO SEE ME WEAR?

WHAT IS YOUR FAVORITE TYPE OF OUTFIT TO SEE ME WEAR?

HOW WOULD YOU DESCRIBE ME IN A PARAGRAPH?

ME

HOW WOULD YOU DESCRIBE ME IN A
PARAGRAPH?

YOU

AT WHAT POINT DID YOU DECIDE YOU WANTED
US TO BE IN AN OFFICIAL RELATIONSHIP?

AT WHAT POINT DID YOU DECIDE YOU WANTED
US TO BE IN AN OFFICIAL RELATIONSHIP?

IF YOU WERE TO GIVE ME A NICKNAME, WHAT WOULD IT BE?

ME

IF YOU WERE TO GIVE ME A NICKNAME, WHAT WOULD IT BE?

YOU

IF YOU COULD TAKE ME AWAY FOR A
WEEKEND, WHERE WOULD IT BE?

ME

IF YOU COULD TAKE ME AWAY FOR A
WEEKEND, WHERE WOULD IT BE?

IF YOU COULD WRITE A SONG ABOUT ME, WHAT WOULD THE TITLE BE AND WHAT WOULD IT BE ABOUT?

ME

IF YOU COULD WRITE A SONG ABOUT ME, WHAT WOULD THE TITLE BE AND WHAT WOULD IT BE ABOUT?

YOU

WHAT IS YOUR ROMANTIC "DREAM" DESTINATION?

ME

WHAT IS YOUR ROMANTIC "DREAM" DESTINATION?

YOU

WHAT IS OUR LOVE SONG?

ME

WHAT IS OUR LOVE SONG?

WHAT IS ONE THING ABOUT ME THAT YOU NEVER GET TIRED OF?

ME

WHAT IS ONE THING ABOUT ME THAT YOU NEVER GET TIRED OF?

YOU

WHICH ONE OF MY NICKNAMES FOR YOU IS
YOUR FAVORITE?

ME

WHICH ONE OF MY NICKNAMES FOR YOU IS YOUR FAVORITE?

YOU

WHAT ARE YOUR GOALS FOR OUR RELATIONSHIP?

ME

WHAT ARE YOUR GOALS FOR OUR RELATIONSHIP?

WHAT HAS BEEN THE HIGHEST POINT OF OUR RELATIONSHIP?

ME

WHAT HAS BEEN THE HIGHEST POINT OF OUR RELATIONSHIP?

WHAT HAS BEEN THE LOWEST POINT OF OUR RELATIONSHIP? HOW DID WE OVERCOME IT?

ME

WHAT HAS BEEN THE LOWEST POINT OF OUR RELATIONSHIP? HOW DID WE OVERCOME IT?

IF YOU HAD ONE WORD TO DESCRIBE OUR LOVE, WHAT WOULD IT BE?

ME

IF YOU HAD ONE WORD TO DESCRIBE OUR
LOVE, WHAT WOULD IT BE?

WHAT ARE 3 DIFFERENCES BETWEEN US THAT YOU LOVE?

WHAT ARE 3 DIFFERENCES BETWEEN US THAT YOU LOVE?

YOU

WHAT'S ONE MAJOR SIMILARITY BETWEEN US
THAT YOU LOVE?

ME

WHAT'S ONE MAJOR SIMILARITY BETWEEN US
THAT YOU LOVE?

YOU

WHAT'S ONE FLAW THAT I SEE ABOUT MYSELF
THAT YOU LOVE?

ME

WHAT'S ONE FLAW THAT I SEE ABOUT MYSELF
THAT YOU LOVE?

THE END

Printed in Great Britain
by Amazon

37891130R00056